DENNY THE DENTIST

by William A Billy III

This Book Belongs to:

____

“Time to brush your teeth!” Mom says after Zane and Kamri get into their pajamas.

BRUSH BRUSH BRUSH

SCRUB SCRUB SCRUB

"Goodnight! Sleep Tight! Don't let the sugar bugs bite."

"What are sugar bugs?" Kamri thought.

"They can bite?" Zane worried.

"Time to brush your teeth!" Dad says as Zane and Kamri wake up the next day.

But Kamri and Zane didn't want to brush.

"We just brushed our teeth last night," they say.

"But what about those sugar bugs?" their mommy asks. "They love making cavity-homes in your teeth."

"Cavities?" Kamri and Zane didn't want those. They knew cavities meant going to the dentist.

"Plus, you need to brush extra well this morning, because you have a dentist appointment today," Dad says.

"The dentist?" Zane and Kamri yelped together. "No!"

They had never been before. They imagine it's like a scary haunted house with loud drills, scary monsters, and sharp tools.

"I don't want to go!" Zane says in a tiny, scared voice.

"I'm too scared to go anywhere!" Kamri adds.

When they arrive, they see a big blue sign.

It's bright, and there's a giant golden treasure chest by the front door.

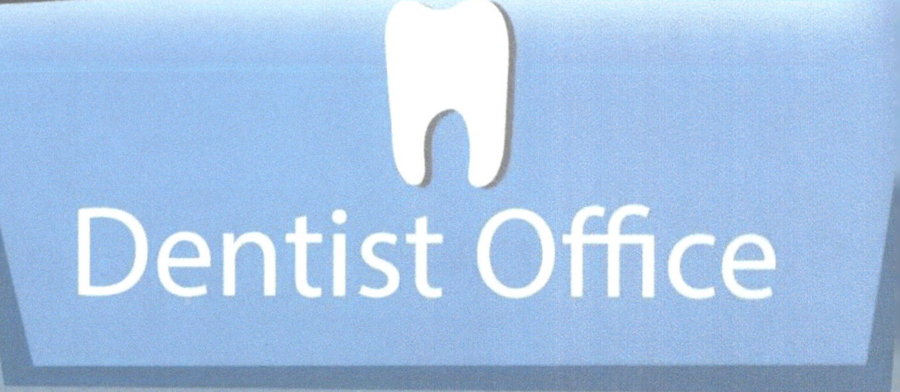

Zane and Kamri look at each other.

“Where are the monsters and loud drills?” Kamri whispers.

“Where are the cobwebs and dark hallways?” Zane shrugs.

"Welcome! Do you want to pick a toothpaste flavor?" a bright-eyed, rosy-cheeked woman asks.

Zane and Kamri were curious. "We have a ton of fun flavors. What's your favorite?" she asks again with a smile.

Zane and Kamri were convinced he was going to look like Dracula. But he didn't.

Denny the Dentist was actually dressed like a wacky clown. And he had a few tricks up his sleeve, too.

He checked their teeth while performing several magic tricks.

Zane and Kamri didn't even realize he was checking their teeth.

Denny was a great dentist and always helped his clients feel comfortable.

"Wow! Kamri, you have wonderful, clean teeth. Not a sugar bug to be found," Denny said with a smile and trick handshake.

"And Zane, you must be a super brusher, because you also have super clean teeth," Denny the Dentist says.

Kamri and Zane felt proud.

“You are both cavity-free! That means you get to pick from the Treasure Chest of Clean Teeth,” Denny says.

Zane and Kamri were excited. Not only was the dentist not scary, but it was kind of fun.

"See you soon! But not too soon!" Denny the Dentist says as he heads off to see his next patients. "Remember, sugar bugs are never fun! But the dentist is!"

Zane and Kamri giggle, thinking about the scary haunted dentist office they thought they were walking into.

"When's our next appointment?" Kamri and Zane ask Dad as they head home.

What is she holding?

What activity is this?

What activity is he doing?

Color the fruits

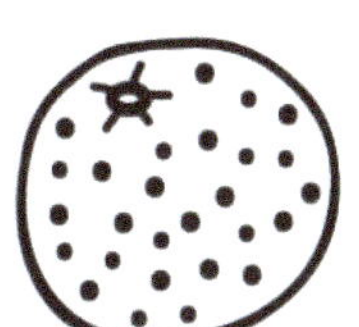

Complete the drawing

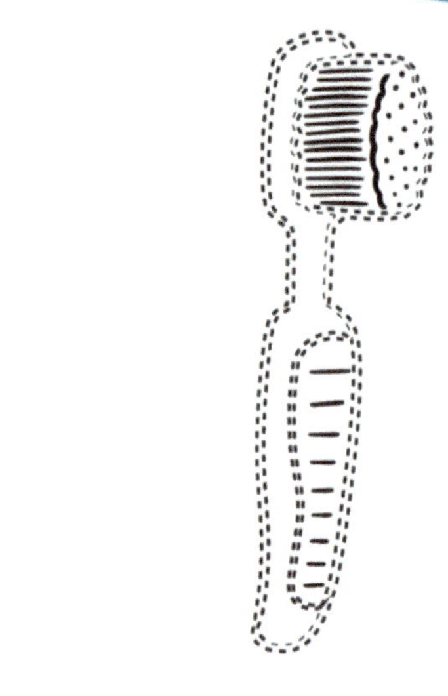

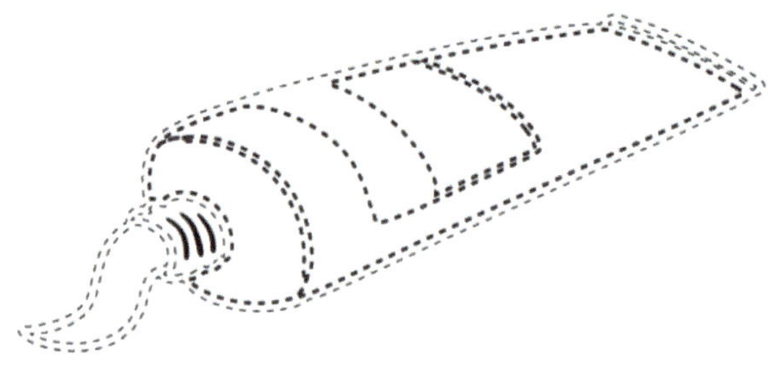

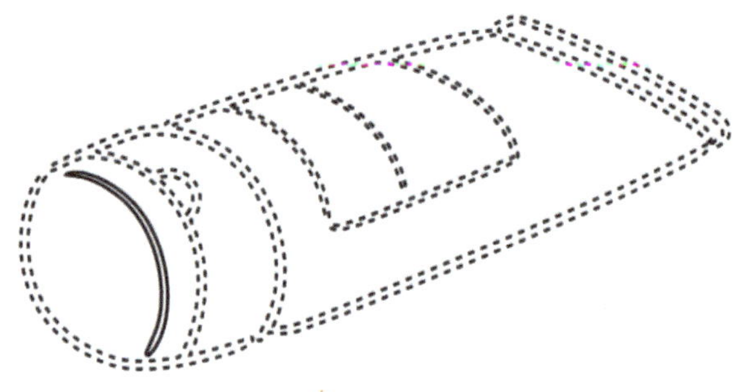

Match the numbers

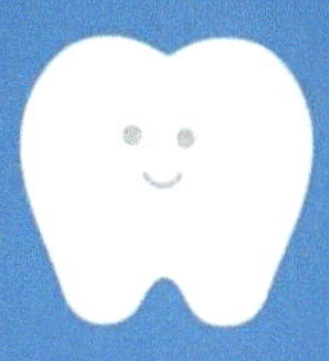

3

7

4

5

6

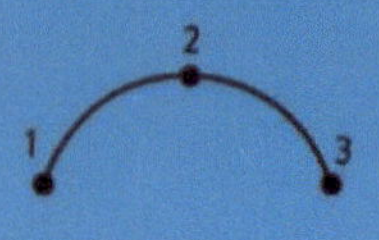

Connect the dots

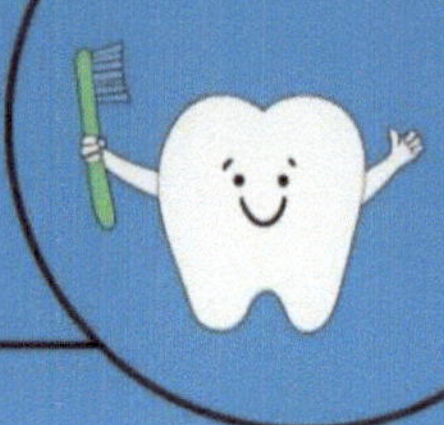

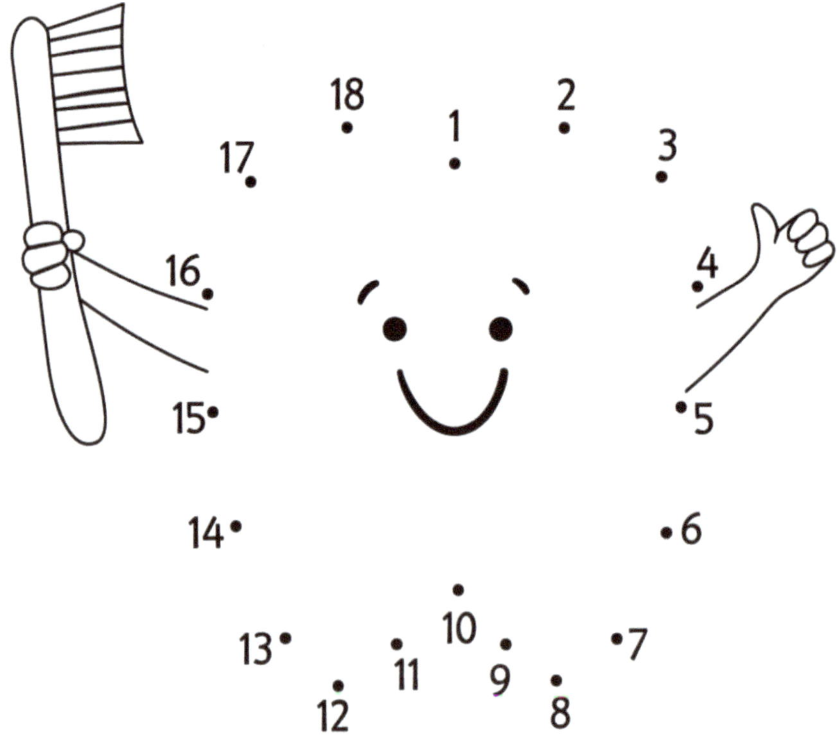

www.ingramcontent.com/pod-product-compliance
Lightning Source LLC
LaVergne TN
LVHW021355160826
845679LV00008B/1630

* 9 7 9 8 3 6 6 5 3 0 2 4 8 *